Pebble® Plus

Understanding Differences

Some Kids Are
Deaf

Revised Edition

Lola M Schaefer

Raintree is an imprint of Capstone Global Library Limited, a company incorporated in England and Wales having its registered office at 264 Banbury Road, Oxford, OX2 7DY – Registered company number: 6695582

www.raintree.co.uk
myorders@raintree.co.uk

Text © Capstone Global Library Limited 2018

Editorial credits
Sarah Bennett, designer; Tracy Cummins, media researcher; Laura Manthe, production specialist

Photo credits
Capstone: 12; Capstone Studio: Karon Dubke, 5, 9, 13, 15, 17, 19; Science Source: Life in View, 11, Spencer Grant, 7; Shutterstock: adriaticfoto, Cover, Andrey_Popov, 21

Printed and bound in India

ISBN 978 1 4747 5688 4 (hardback)
ISBN 978 1 4747 9232 5 (paperback)

British Library Cataloguing in Publication Data

A full catalogue record for this book is available from the British Library.

Every effort has been made to contact copyright holders of material reproduced in this book. Any omissions will be rectified in subsequent printings if notice is given to the publisher.

All the Internet addresses (URLs) given in this book were valid at the time of going to press. However, due to the dynamic nature of the Internet, some addresses may have changed, or sites may have changed or ceased to exist since publication. While the author and publisher regret any inconvenience this may cause readers, no responsibility for any such changes can be accepted by either the author or the publisher.

Contents

Deafness

Some kids are deaf.

Kids who are deaf

cannot hear.

Some kids are born deaf.

Other kids become deaf

from an illness

or from getting injured.

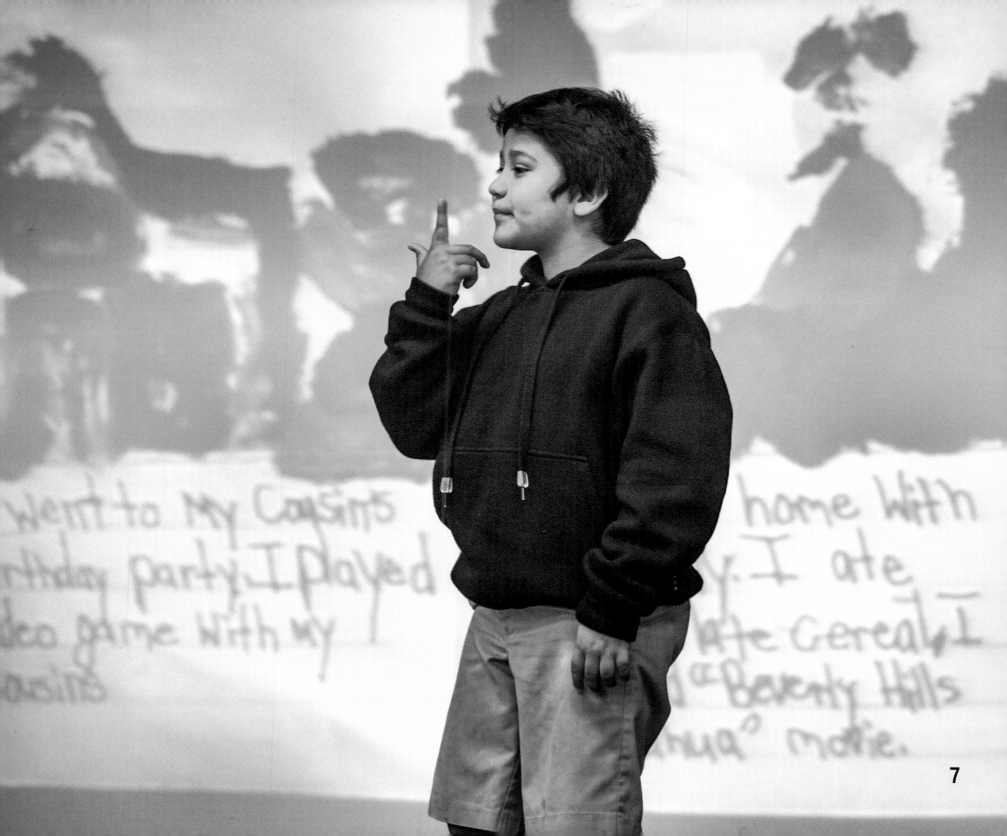

Tools for hearing

Some kids can hear a little.

They wear hearing aids

to hear sounds louder.

Some kids who are deaf get cochlear implants. Implants help them hear some sounds.

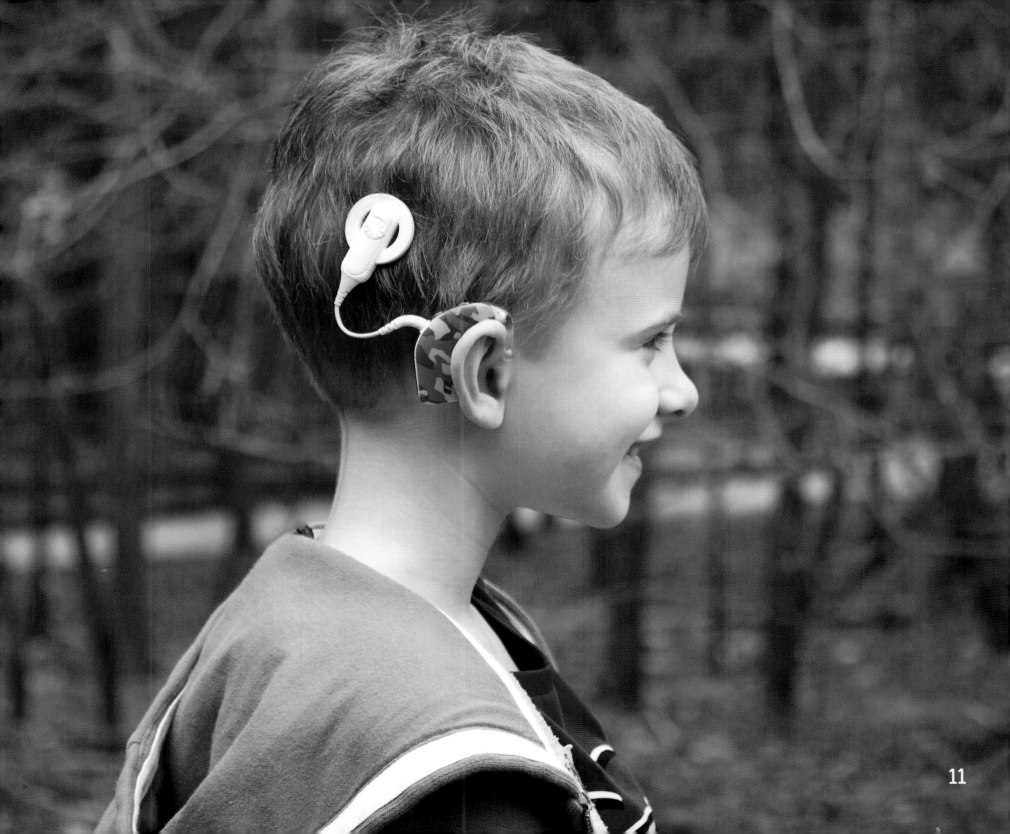

Talking

Some kids who are deaf
use sign language to talk.
Sign language is hand signs
that stand for letters, words
and numbers.

Sign Language

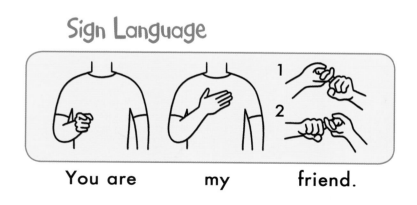

You are   my   friend.

Some kids who are deaf
use their voice to talk.
Speech therapists teach
them to speak clearly.

Everyday life

Kids who are deaf depend on their sense of sight. Flashing lights tell them it's time for class.

Kids who are deaf watch TV
with subtitles.
The words tell what people
on TV are saying.

TV G
MACAPA
AMAZON BASIN
BRAZIL
STRADDLING THE EQUATOR,
MACAPA, BRAZIL IS AN EXOTIC WORLD
ORION
MTS STEREO

Kids who are deaf depend on
their sense of touch.
They can feel a phone
vibrate when a friend sends
a text message.

Glossary

cochlear implant small electronic device that is surgically
put into a person's head; cochlear implants allow sounds to
get to the brain

deaf being unable to hear

hearing aid small electronic device that people wear in or behind one or
both ears; hearing aids make sounds louder

senses ways of learning about your surroundings; hearing, smelling,
touching, tasting and sight are the five senses

sign language hand signs that stand for words, letters
and numbers

speech therapist person who is trained to help people
learn to speak clearly

text message words sent from a mobile phone to another person's mobile
phone

Find out more

Books

Proud to be Deaf, Ava, Lilli and Nick Beese (Wayland, 2017)

Having a Disability (Questions and Feelings About), Louise Spilsbury (Franklin Watts, 2017)

We All Have Different Abilities (Celebrating Differences), Melissa Higgins (Raintree, 2017)

Websites

Watch a video about how a deaf boy uses sign language to communicate: https://www.bbc.co.uk/education/clips/zc676sg

Find out what it's like to be deaf and how you can help communicate with deaf people: http://www.signhealth.org.uk/about-deafness/deaf-awareness/

Comprehension questions

1. What other senses are helpful to a person who is deaf?

2. Describe sign language.

3. How do flashing lights at school help children who are deaf?

Index